my itty-bitty bio

Marian Anderson

Published in the United States of America by Cherry Lake Publishing
Ann Arbor, Michigan
www.cherrylakepublishing.com

Content Adviser: Ryan Emery Hughes, Doctoral Student, School of Education, University of Michigan
Reading Adviser: Marla Conn MS, Ed., Literacy specialist, Read-Ability, Inc.
Book Design: Jennifer Wahi
Illustrator: Jeff Bane

Photo Credits: © Marian Anderson used with permission from the Family of James DePriest, 5, 19; © chetpatchet/ Shutterstock, 7, 22; © Everett Collection Historical / Alamy Stock Photo, 9; © Carl Van Vechten/Library of Congress, 11, 21; © Harris & Ewing/Library of Congress, 13; © World History Archive / Alamy Stock Photo, 15, 23; © U.S. Information Agency/National Archives and Records Administration, page 17; Cover, 8, 14, 18, Jeff Bane; Various frames throughout, Shutterstock Images

Library of Congress Cataloging-in-Publication Data

Names: Haldy, Emma E.
Title: Marian Anderson / Emma E. Haldy.
Description: Ann Arbor, Michigan : Cherry Lake Publishing, 2016. | Series: My itty-bitty bio | Includes bibliographical references and index.
Identifiers: LCCN 2015046418| ISBN 9781634710237 (hardcover) | ISBN 9781634711227 (pdf) | ISBN 9781634712217 (pbk.) | ISBN 9781634713207 (ebook)
Subjects: LCSH: Anderson, Marian, 1897-1993--Juvenile literature. | Contraltos--United States--Biography--Juvenile literature. | African American singers--Biography--Juvenile literature. | LCGFT: Biographies.
Classification: LCC ML3930.A5 H37 2016 | DDC 782.1092--dc23
LC record available at http://lccn.loc.gov/2015046418

Printed in the United States of America
Corporate Graphics

table of contents

About the author: Emma E. Haldy is a former librarian and a proud Michigander. She lives with her husband, Joe, and an ever-growing collection of books.

About the illustrator: Jeff Bane and his two business partners own a studio along the American River in Folsom, California, home of the 1849 Gold Rush. When Jeff's not sketching or illustrating for clients, he's either swimming or kayaking in the river to relax.

I was born in 1897.

I had two sisters.
My family was poor.

I was good at singing. I sang in my church choir.

My church believed in me. They found me a teacher. I became a great singer.

What is your favorite song?

I won a contest to sing with the New York **Philharmonic**. I became famous.

I sang all over the world. I was one of the best singers of my time.

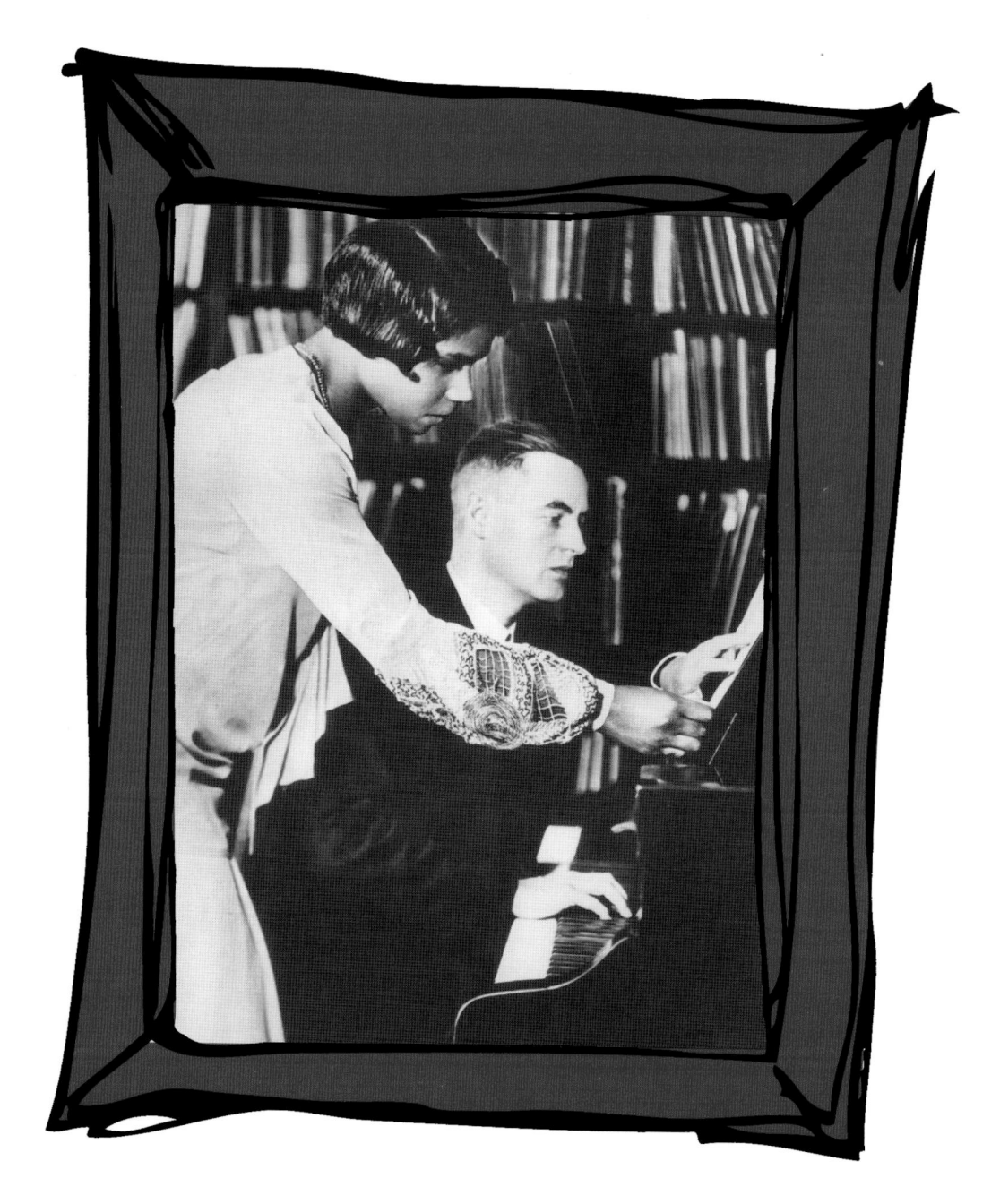

But I was black. I faced **racism** in America. I could not sing everywhere.

It made me unhappy. I was an artist. I wanted to share my gift.

I asked to sing in **Constitution Hall**. I was refused. Only white performers were allowed.

People found out. They got upset. Even First Lady Eleanor Roosevelt was mad.

She invited me to sing at the **Lincoln Memorial**.

I sang for 75,000 people.

Millions listened on the radio.
They were white and black.
It was an important day.

I inspired people. I gave them hope. I kept singing.

I sang in the White House. I sang for soldiers during **World War II**. I sang at the **Metropolitan Opera**.

Who inspires you?

I sang less as I got older.
I worked to help my community.
I wrote a book.

I was honored with many awards. I died in 1993.

I was a talented woman. I never gave up. I showed people that music does not have a color.

What would you like to ask me?

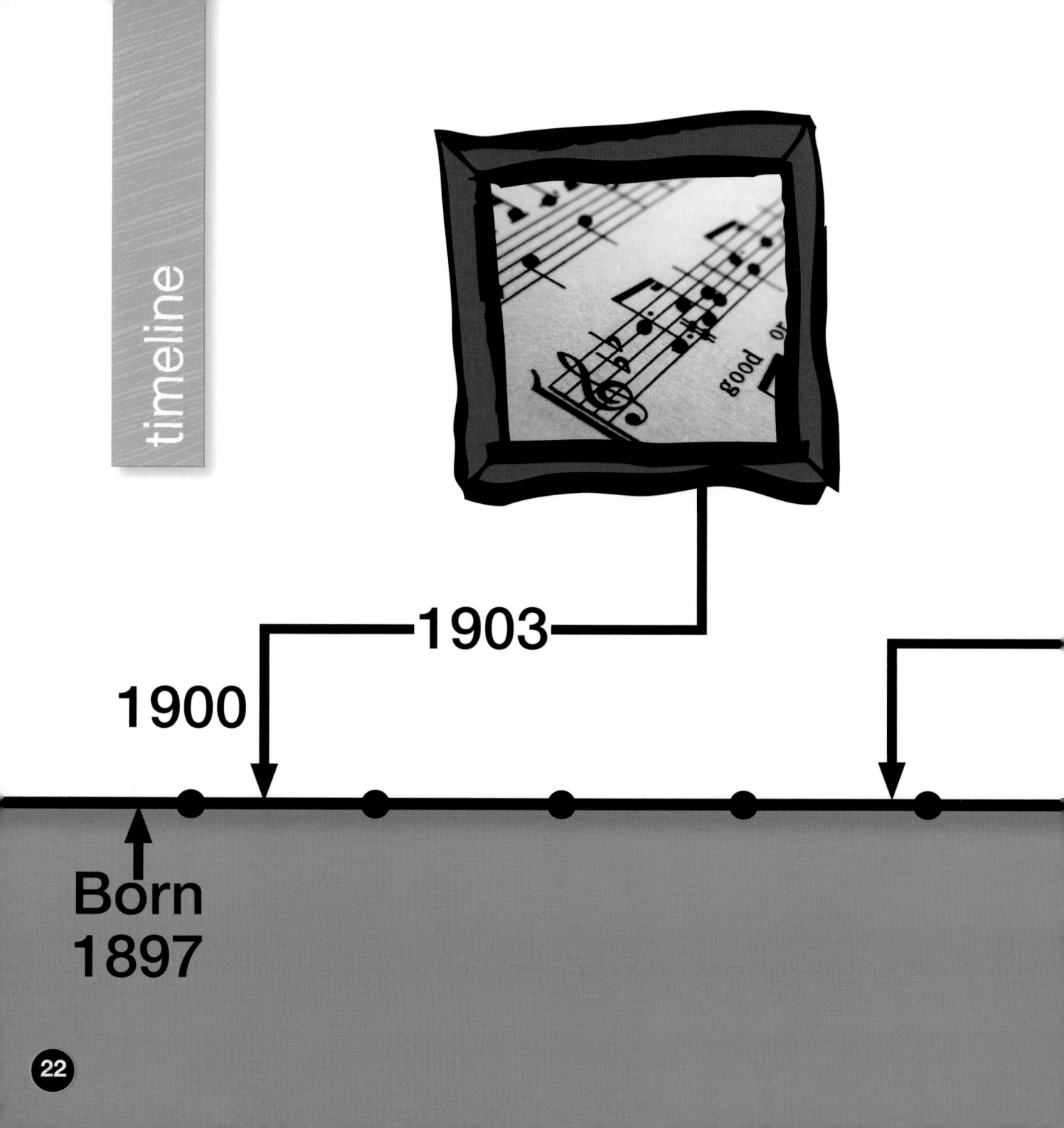

1903

1900

Born
1897

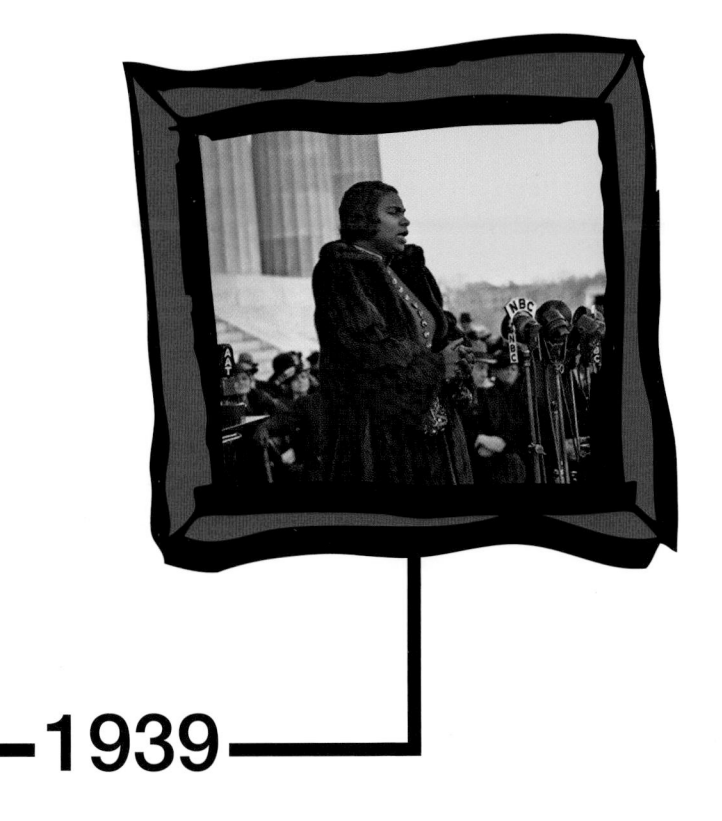

1939

2000

↑
Died
1993

glossary

Constitution Hall (kahn-sti-TOO-shuhn HAWL) a large music hall in Washington, D.C.

Lincoln Memorial (LING-kuhn muh-MOR-ee-uhl) a monument to honor President Abraham Lincoln

Metropolitan Opera (met-ruh-PAH-li-tuhn AH-pur-uh) a famous music hall in New York City

Philharmonic (fil-har-MON-ik) a large group of musicians who play different instruments

racism (RAY-siz-uhm) the belief that one race is better than another

World War II (WURLD WOR TOO) a war fought overseas from 1939 to 1945

index